SCIENTOLOGY
Making the World a Better Place

Founded and developed by L. Ron Hubbard, Scientology is an applied religious philosophy which offers an exact route through which anyone can regain the truth and simplicity of his spiritual self.

Scientology consists of specific axioms that define the underlying causes and principles of existence and a vast area of observations in the humanities, a philosophic body that literally applies to the entirety of life.

This broad body of knowledge resulted in two applications of the subject: first, a technology for man to increase his spiritual awareness and attain the freedom sought by many great philosophic teachings; and, second, a great number of fundamental principles men can use to improve their lives. In fact, in this second application, Scientology offers nothing less than practical methods to better *every* aspect of our existence—means to create new ways of life. And from this comes the subject matter you are about to read.

Compiled from the writings of L. Ron Hubbard, the data presented here is but one of the tools which can be found in *The Scientology Handbook*. A comprehensive guide, the handbook contains numerous applications of Scientology which can be used to improve many other areas of life.

In this booklet, the editors have augmented the data with a short introduction, practical exercises and examples of successful application.

Courses to increase your understanding and further materials to broaden your knowledge are available at your nearest Scientology church or mission, listed at the back of this booklet.

Many new phenomena about man and life are described in Scientology, and so you may encounter terms in these pages you are not familiar with. These are described the first time they appear and in the glossary at the back of the booklet.

Scientology is for use. It is a practical philosophy, something one *does*. Using this data, you *can* change conditions.

Millions of people who want to do something about the conditions they see around them have applied this knowledge. They know that life can be improved. And they know that Scientology works.

Use what you read in these pages to help yourself and others and you will too.

CHURCH OF SCIENTOLOGY INTERNATIONAL

We live in a perilous world, a dangerous environment. Watch television news or read your daily newspaper and you are subjected to a daily diet of robberies, rapes, riots, murders, fires, earthquakes, floods and famines.

Do you find yourself becoming disturbed by what is happening around you? Do you feel helpless, unable to control these events? Do you even sometimes feel afraid?

In this booklet, L. Ron Hubbard dissects this phenomenon of the dangerous environment, providing methods that will not only help you overcome your fears, but allow you to help others. Applied on a broad scale, this information brings about an enormous calming influence and enables people to lead happier lives. Used on an individual scale—by you—it will enhance the lives of your family, friends and associates. ■

The Dangerous Environment

Many people are not only convinced that the environment is dangerous, but that it is steadily growing more so. For many, it's more of a challenge than they feel up to.

The fact of the matter is, however, that the environment is *made* to appear much more dangerous than it actually is.

A great number of people are professional dangerous environment *makers*. This includes professions which require a dangerous environment for their existence such as the politician, the policeman, the newspaperman, the undertaker and others. These people sell a dangerous environment. That is their mainstay. They feel that if they did not sell people on the idea the environment is dangerous, they would promptly go broke. So it is in their interest to make the environment far more dangerous than it is.

The environment is dangerous enough.

At one time an idea was put forth that certain societies did not advance because the environment lacked sufficient challenge. One of those advancing the idea was English historian and philosopher Arnold Toynbee (1889–1975) who felt that areas such as Mexico did not progress for that reason. Toynbee's idea on this, however, was born in an ivory tower environment, sitting in libraries reading books, but never going out and talking to any Mexicans.

So Toynbee pronounced with great conclusive exclamation points followed by innumerable university degrees, "The reason the Mexican does not succeed is he has insufficient challenge in his environment. The reason South America isn't an up-and-coming industrial power is insufficient challenge in the environment. The reason the African has not progressed further in civilization is because his environment has insufficient challenge."

What did Toynbee know of it? He spent all his time in the back end of a library, reading books written by men who had spent all of *their* days in libraries! That is no way to learn about life.

In the Philippines, for an added example, a bold, energetic white man arrives and he advises the native Igorots—a tribe which inhabits the northern mountainous region of the Philippines. He says, "If you will just cut a pathway from the village down to the river, then take a bullock cart down to the river in the morning and fill up a water tank and bring it back to the village, your women won't have to be making that long walk to the river. You should engage upon this public works project at once."

He becomes absolutely *outraged* that they don't immediately act on his suggestion and he goes away, thinking, "Aha! Those people have insufficient challenge in the environment. Nothing for them to measure up to. No ambition. Not like us in the West—we have challenge in our environment."

This man had challenge in his environment? Mama spooned Wheaties into his mouth, Papa wrote all the checks as he went through college and his way was paved in all directions with machinery and vehicles. His environment was already licked, so of course he could afford to be bold.

But what really is the environment of the Igorot as he sits by the fire, listening to the white man tell him how he has to cut a path to the river? This Igorot has a little boy, whom he loves very much, but he knows this little boy has only a slim chance of living until he is seven due to disease and bad food. He knows that when the rains come, they won't just be pleasant light rains; they will flood every seed out of the ground and pound the fields to pieces but *if* he can salvage anything out of that, maybe he will live a few more months. He knows all he has to do is walk under the wrong tree and get hit by a poisonous snake, and that will be the end of him. In other words, he already knows he cannot live, so why try?

In other words, the challenge of the environment is absolutely overwhelming for many people.

But does this mean there is no challenge in the environment in the more "civilized" parts of the world? By no means. Consider the situation of a young artist from Terre Haute, Indiana, who moved to New York City. The casual observer might say that he moved because there was no challenge in his environment in Terre Haute. No, here again, the challenge was too much.

This fellow decided to become a painter in the first place because he couldn't face working in the feed store with the same fellow who beat him up during kindergarten, beat him up during grammar school and beat him up in high school. The thought of having to work with this fellow every day was just too much challenge for him. So he became an artist, but nobody in Terre Haute bought paintings and nobody believed in what he was doing. He had no future there; he was facing continual starvation, he was unable to contribute to his community. That was a very hostile environment. So he moved to a friendlier one, Greenwich Village. He would rather starve to death quietly in Greenwich Village than be threatened to death in Terre Haute, Indiana.

We come to the conclusion, then, that any individual—whether white, black, red or yellow—if he has not been able to achieve his own destiny, must be in an environment that he finds overwhelming, and his methods of taking care of that environment must be inadequate to his survival. His existence is as apathetic or as unhappy as his environment seems to him to be overwhelming.

Why then would people go out of their way to actually make the environment appear more dangerous than it already is?

The Merchants of Chaos

There are those who could be called "merchants of chaos." These are people who want an environment to look very, very disturbing. These are people who gain some sort of advantage, they feel, if the environment is made to look more threatening.

An obvious example can be seen in newspapers. There are no good news stories. Newspapermen shove the environment in people's faces and say, "Look! It's dangerous. Look! It's overwhelming. Look! It's threatening." They not only report the most threatening bits of news, but also sensationalize it, making it worse than it is. What more do you want as a proof of their intention? This is the merchant of chaos. He is paid to the degree that he can make the environment threatening. To yearn for good news is foolhardy in a society where the merchants of chaos reign.

The chaos merchant has lots of troops among people with vested interests.

And do not think it an accident that the current justice system will take a dangerous criminal, throw him into prison, make him more antisocial and more dangerous and then release him upon the society. The more crime, the more police are needed.

Ideas of this kind are found in the society to a marked degree. It isn't just the newspaper reporter or the politician; individuals here and there also engage upon this.

A lot of people spend their whole lives as professional chaos merchants; they worry those around them to death. The percentage who do this may be as high as one out of four. For example, a housewife, operating as a merchant of chaos in her sphere of influence, thinks of her husband, "If I can just keep Henry worried enough, he will do what I tell him." She operates on the idea that it is necessary to spread confusion and upset. But along with this goes a concern, "I wonder why Henry doesn't get ahead?" Naturally, she is making him sick.

The truth of the matter, however, is this: the environment is not as dangerous, ever, as it is made to appear. Instead, tremendous numbers of people and vast amounts of money are manufacturing a dangerous environment. In fact, in the 1960s a huge proportion of the national budget of the United States was dedicated to atomic war. But if they hadn't developed the threat, there would not have been one. The money that financed the horror was busy supporting the horror.

It is not to the advantage of those who get their income, appropriations or public interest from the amount of disturbance to make a peaceful environment.

A Calming Influence

Anything that tends to pacify or bring a calmed environment is resisted by the vested interest that backs a disturbed environment.

To the degree Scientology progresses in an area, the environment becomes calmer and calmer. Not less adventurous, but calmer. In other words, the potential hostile, unreachable, untouchable threat in the environment reduces. Somebody who knows more about himself, others and life, and who gets a better grip on situations, has less trouble in his environment. Even though it may only be reduced slightly, it is reduced.

Newspapers can have a depressing effect on a person.

Since they deal largely in bad news, they present a generally bleak picture of the world.

One can carry the bad news around with him and get a negatively distorted idea of his surroundings, which may, in reality, actually be quite calm.

Even somebody who has heard very little of Scientology has less turmoil in his environment. An individual, less threatened by the environment, tends to resurge. He gets less apathetic. He thinks he can do more about life. He can reach outward a little further; therefore he can exert a calming influence upon his immediate environment.

As that progressed forward, more and more individuals would be produced who could bring more and more calm to the environment or handle things better and better. It is only the things which aren't handled which are chaotic. It would result in a situation where the threat of the environment would die out. This overwhelming, overpowering environment would be tamer and tamer. People would be less and less afraid. You would have more and more opportunity of handling the actual problems that exist instead of people dreaming up problems in order to make some money off of it. It would be a different society.

The merchant of chaos does not like calming influences, however. He will fight anything which lessens disturbance in the environment.

For example, a wife has her husband completely under her thumb. She keeps him worried and upset morning, noon and night.

If the husband now engages in some activity which brings more calmness to the environment, there will be repercussions from the wife. If he is less disturbed, he is less under her control. She would naturally fight the thing that was making her husband more calm.

Yet disturbance and chaos fold up in the face of truth. It is lies which keep the universe continuously disturbed. The introduction of truth into a society would produce a calmer environment with less disturbance and therefore less that could be swindled out of that society by merchants of chaos.

Ways to Lessen the Threat

People are looking for a less threatening environment, or at least for a way to better endure the environment they live in.

The concept of the dangerous environment will be understandable to the individual no matter how crudely it is put to him. Just the concept that he considers the environment dangerous and overwhelming and he doesn't quite know where that danger or overwhelm is coming from is an enormous piece of wisdom.

Shrinking back from a very threatening environment that may overwhelm him at any moment, unable to progress forward into greater endurance or power to handle that threatening environment—this is his life.

An individual's health level, sanity level, activity level and ambition level are all monitored by *his* concept of the dangerousness of the environment.

There *are* real areas of danger in the environment, but there are also areas being made to *seem* more dangerous than they really are.

Thus, if a person is marched forward into these sectors of his environment and gotten to inspect them, he can perceive for himself that the environment is not as dangerous as it is being made to seem. And with increased confidence in his ability to handle at least *those* sectors of his environment, his health, well-being, sanity and activity levels will rise as well.

A number of simple procedures can help a person increase his command over his environment. The master question of all these techniques is "What part of the environment isn't threatening?" If one can get him to differentiate and find out there are some parts of the environment that *aren't* threatening, he will make considerable gain.

What is the individual's expectancy at this level? It may be this low—that he just won't be so frightened when the doorbell rings. This sounds like a tiny improvement; nevertheless, it would be quite real to him.

He might just want to handle it so that when he wakes up in the morning he doesn't have an agonizing feeling that something horrible is going to happen if he gets out of bed—and maybe he doesn't even expect that feeling to completely disappear, but hopes it will diminish.

These would be real gains to him, and he would be very happy with them. The funny thing is, the gains he will actually experience will, in most cases, greatly exceed expectations.

Here are the procedures you can use to accomplish this:

1. Find Something That Isn't Being a Threat

When a person gets too upset or confused, one can have him look around his environment and find something that isn't being a threat to him. Carry on doing this until the person is very happy or relieved and has had a realization about himself, the environment or life in general.

A person can also use this technique directly on himself. For example, an individual can be in his office and very worried about something. He may be sitting at his desk with papers piling up. Everything seems to be in a high uproar, and he feels completely overwhelmed. The person himself ought to be able to look at the papers on his desk (the source of the threat) and find something about them that is not a threat. By making such a discovery, the threat will balance out.

2. Don't Read the Newspaper

This is very simple. Tell the person, "**Don't read the newspapers for two weeks and see if you don't feel better.**"

If he doesn't read the newspapers for two weeks, of course he will feel better.

Then tell him, "**Now read the newspaper for a week, and at the end of that week you will find you feel worse. Then make up your mind whether or not you ought to pay any attention to the newspapers.**"

This could be proposed to the person as a simple experiment. It isn't even an expensive experiment—as a matter of fact, it is cheaper *not* to buy newspapers than to buy them.

This is a simple action, but a very effective one which can markedly change a person's outlook on life.

3. Take a Walk

Another way of having a person look at the environment and discover that it isn't so threatening is a technique called "**Take a Walk.**" If a person feels bad, have him take a walk and look at things as he walks.

The effort here is just to get the individual to inspect the environment and find out that there is some slightly greater security in it. One just wants the person to look and find out if the environment is as threatening as it appears to be.

"Take a walk and look at things" is the mildest advice that you could possibly give anybody, and is almost certain to produce a result if the person will do it. It is quite effective.

4. Find Something That Isn't Hostile to You

There are people who feel as if everybody in the environment is hostile to them.

For a person like this, there is another technique that will lessen his fears.

One could ask any of several different questions, depending upon the situation. Examples of these are:

"Find something people say or do around here that isn't hostile to you."

"Is there one person in the company who isn't actively hostile to you?"

"Is there anything said today that wasn't directly and immediately hostile to you?"

Ask the person one of the above questions (or a similar question with a wording more appropriate to the person's situation). For example, ask him, "Is there one person in the company who isn't actively hostile to you?"

Continue this until the person feels better, is happier and has had a realization about himself, the environment or life in general.

5. Handling a Loss

A fellow who has just lost his girl, or a woman who has lost her man, feels the horrible sadness and loss it imparts to everything. Actually, everything in the environment will "talk" to him or her about the lost love. For some period of time, it will be impossible for him to look around and not be reminded of this person.

When one's concentration has been heavily on an individual, it is sometimes almost heroically difficult to not associate everything with that person. The trick is to find something that isn't reminding the person of the one he or she lost. One might have to search a long way to find something.

This is the way to recover from a love affair. The situation is in actual fact a simple one: the individual has identified everything in the environment with his unrest. By directing the person's attention to things in the environment which are not so connected and making him find things which are not actively reminding him, one gets a *differentiation* where an *identification* existed before. And where differentiation exists, intelligence and judgment can return.

Do the following:

Tell the person you are going to help them. Tell him or her, "**Find something that isn't reminding you of _____ (name of person he or she lost).**"

Repeat the command, getting the person to find something else that is not reminding him or her of the person until he or she has a realization and feels better about the situation.

This simple procedure can help the person recover from his or her lost love and begin to live again.

6. Arranging One's Life

By having an individual plan a life by which he could live calmly and unthreatened, the life he is living becomes less threatening.

Let us take, for example, the poor fellow who is on a complete treadmill: he has to keep his job, even though it doesn't pay enough and there's no opportunity of advancement, because if he loses it, he feels he won't be able to get another one or he won't be able to survive. This man is in a box of his own making, and he finds that environment very hostile.

Get him to plan a life which would not be so threatening, no matter how imaginative or seemingly unattainable his plan, and he will be able to go on working at his job much more happily and feeling much calmer.

7. Knocking Off Things That Upset One

There is another action which consists of simply having the person stop doing things or associating with people that upset him.

One could say, "**Knock off some of those things in your life that make you upset.**"

"Who upsets you? Well, don't talk to them for a while."

"What activities leave you feeling worse? Well, just don't do them for a while."

"What things in the environment *aren't* really a threat to you? All right, have you got some of those? Fine. **Associate with those. Pay more attention to them.**"

This will benefit the person more than one might imagine.

A broken love affair can result in the person being in a state of mind where everything in the environment is a reminder of the loss.

But a person can be helped to recover. If one can find something in the surroundings which does not bring to mind the lost love …

… the person's attention can become unstuck, which allows her to feel better.

CONFRONT

One can safely assume that there is always *something* about a situation the person can confront—by which we mean easily face without flinching.

This is a principle which forms the basis of a solution for many who are overwhelmed by their environments.

For example, a social worker is visiting Mrs. O'Leary in her tenement. Mrs. O'Leary has an awful lot of problems and she is telling them to the social worker: her husband gets drunk all the time and never brings home any pay and the furniture is all broken and the children have no clothes and it's impossible to keep the place clean and so forth.

The social worker can really get somewhere if he can find something that can be confronted by the person he is trying to help and get him to actually do it. Although this sounds very simple and innocuous, it has fantastic workability.

People working in the field of social work usually fail to simply adjudicate the problems involved in the situation and then do something about those problems that *can* have something done about them and that somebody *can* confront to do something about them. So as a net result, a social worker doesn't succeed because he never gives anybody anything they can do.

The well-meaning social worker says, "What you want to do, Mrs. O'Leary, is clean this whole place up, scrub it down from top to bottom—after all, we've given you soap. And get your children cleaned up and put in those nice new dresses we sent you. Now, I'll have a talk with your husband concerning his drinking."

At this point, even if Mrs. O'Leary *would* have cleaned up the whole place and put the children in the clean clothes, she and the social worker part company violently. The social worker has just told Mrs. O'Leary something that she *knows* by experience *cannot be done*. Nobody can talk to her husband about his drinking. She doesn't think that even a full-scale attack by the United States Army could do anything about Mr. O'Leary's drinking. Nothing the social worker does or says from this point on is going to have any effect on Mrs. O'Leary.

Suppose, however, that the social worker listened carefully to Mrs. O'Leary and then applied the principle of giving her something she could actually confront handling. He might have noticed that during their conversation, Mrs. O'Leary had emptied an ashtray for his cigarette. So he says to her, "I'll tell you what I would do. I would start in on this thing a little bit at a time, and I would get the place cleaned up. Now, why don't you keep the ashtrays emptied?" She might even get angry with him, but when the social worker leaves, Mrs. O'Leary will go around and empty the ashtrays.

Finding something that the person can confront handling is essential to getting his or her agreement to handle it. The first level of help is "There is something to be done about it," and the second level contains the element, *"that you can do."* Giving a person something he or she can confront and actually get done starts to give him the idea that the situation can be handled. The next thing you know, Mrs. O'Leary is liable to start getting ideas that she can even do something to make her husband stop drinking.

This principle of giving a person something they can confront doing is fabulously useful in many areas.

People often don't know how to get any further along in life. They *know* they cannot make any improvement in life, that it is impossible to be any better at all. But using this datum, one could easily demonstrate, even to a whole group, that it *is* possible to get better. It would be done in the following manner:

Start by advising the person you want to help, "**Write down on a piece of paper a short list of the problems you have in your life.**"

When he has done that, ask, "**Which one of those is the easiest for you to confront? Now write that down.**"

A person may be in a situation which seems overwhelming to him, so he does not do anything about it.

But he can be helped by finding something about the circumstances he can confront handling.

If he can handle one aspect of the situation, his outlook about it can be markedly improved, and he will be able to handle it fully.

Then tell him, "**Write down what you absolutely know for sure you could do about that last thing you wrote down.**"

And finally, tell him, "**Now, you see what you've written down at the bottom of this page? Do it!**"

Use of this principle can be of enormous assistance to people—in social work, in leading groups, in teaching and lecturing and many other areas.

Don't tell people about problems that they know they cannot do anything about and expect them to be enthusiastic about accomplishing anything.

Neither the problem being pointed out nor the suggested solution must exceed the ability to confront on the part of the person to whom it is being addressed. The easiest thing to relay is an idea, but the idea must not violate the potential to confront of the individual who is expected to execute it.

The sequence is: What is the situation? What part of the situation is potentially confrontable? And what part of that situation will somebody do something about?

Most people stop giving advice because the advice they give is never followed. But if one followed the rules laid out here, he would be a very successful adviser.

Since what the people are being asked to do is confrontable to them, they will be able to handle their problems and succeed at it. As a result, they will be able to see and confront more of their difficulties, and the above sequence can be repeated. A new review of the general situation will find that they have an improved idea of what is potentially confrontable amongst their problems.

The only difficulty one can encounter is that people sometimes start moving with too great a confidence and, like a baby who has just learned how to walk, go tearing across the room at a high run. Unfortunately, they usually fall on their faces on about the third step. They can get overly ambitious. That has to be taken into consideration, and the person warned with, "Don't do any more than this right now."

If you make it your business to (1) rapidly get an estimation of what a person thinks is wrong; then (2) find out which one of these points he can confront; then (3) find out what he is going to do about that point that he thinks he can do; and then (4) get him to do it, and at that point you become terribly insistent on the subject of *getting that point done,* you will have agreement with a capital "A" every time.

The Real World

The world simply must not be a better place, according to the chaos merchant. And so long as politicians move upward on scandal, the military establishment gets fatter on more war, and the media profits from the spread of bad news, there will continue to be those who thrive on chaos.

But this is the created world, not the real world. Behind all this upset and disturbance there exists a calmer environment. It is one in which man can live and feel better, a world where people do heroic deeds and neighbors help each other and people overcome vast odds to excel.

The differences between a competent person and an incompetent person are demonstrated in his environment (surroundings). A person is either the effect of his environment or is able to have an effect upon his environment.

The nineteenth-century psychologist preached that man had to "adjust to his environment." This false datum helped begin a racial degeneration.

The truth is that man is as successful as he adjusts the environment to him.

Being competent means the ability to control and operate the things in the environment and the environment itself.

By recognizing the work of the chaos merchant, people can begin to better control their environments.■

Practical Exercises

Here are exercises relating to handling the dangerous environment. Doing these exercises will increase your understanding of how to help people deal with the problems and difficulties in their lives.

1. Look around and find examples where the environment is made to look more dangerous than it really is. Do this until you are certain that the environment is being made to look more dangerous than it really is.

2. Take a walk around the block, looking at things as you walk. After taking the walk, compare how threatening the environment seemed before and how it seems now.

3. Find a friend or family member who is feeling overwhelmed by the environment and help them, using one of the seven techniques given in the section "Ways to Lessen the Threat."

4. Help a person by getting him to write down a short list of the problems he has in his life. Then get him to find which one of those is easiest for him to confront. Get him to write that down. Then get him to write down what he absolutely knows for sure he could do about the last thing he wrote down. Now, get him to take the last thing he wrote down and do it.

Results from Application

L Ron Hubbard has provided simple actions one can take to help others who are overwhelmed by life. People who use these find that they have in their hands very basic but highly effective weapons against the cynical generality or hopeless attitude that "everything is bad everywhere" and there is no hope for man or anything else.

Perhaps the most commented-upon aspect of this activity—helping another become more causative over a dangerous environment—is that it really takes very little to help one's fellow man and give him some hope. This fact is reflected in the stories below.

A woman who had studied Mr. Hubbard's discoveries about how to help someone confront and handle a dangerous environment said this about the technology's effectiveness:

*"My friend came to see me the night after I finished studying this data and she was full of problems that she had no solutions for. Applying L. Ron Hubbard's technology, I asked her to write down a list of things that were problems in her life, then note which one she thought was the easiest to confront. Then I asked her to write down what she knew for **sure** she could do about that one. The effect of these questions was amazing. She immediately got very bright, whereas she had been very depressed when she first walked in. She dashed out to handle the problem at once, though I had never before seen this woman actually attempt to **handle** anything in her life—prior to this she had only complained! I saw once again how, with Scientology, a little goes a long way!"*

Continuously getting overwhelmed in her work was a "normal" part of life for a woman from Omaha, Nebraska, until she received some help from a friend.

"I would habitually build up more and more things to do and never finish any of them. Then after a few weeks I would end up in tears, feeling overwhelmed from 'overwork.' The world would look pretty awful and the people in it would all seem pretty mean to me. A friend told me how to write down a list of my problems, pick out the one I could face, then do something about that. From that point on I gained control over situations just by taking one problem at a time, creatively solving that one and then going on to the next, instead of drowning in how

Dealing With the Future

Facing tomorrow is a distinctly different proposition for those who apply Scientology to their environment than for those who don't.

SURVEY QUESTION: "Do You Dread the Future?"

Non-Scientologists: **Yes 29%**
Scientologists: **Yes 0%**

'impossible' it all seemed. The world did not look so mean after that because I was in charge. This was the first piece of Scientology data anyone had ever applied to me and I have used this in my life ever since. Now I am able to enjoy my work much more."

Unable to tolerate seeing another in distress without doing something about it, a California woman used Mr. Hubbard's technology to help others in trying circumstances. She had many successes with these simple solutions.

"I helped a man and his wife whom I met on the bus one day. The wife was in tears for some reason. I got her to look at those things in the environment which she felt were not hostile to her. She became bright and started working out how she could solve her own problems. Another time I helped a man, who had been very upset and hysterical in his environment, to move to a new place and to take daily walks. He became much saner and started to reach out and help others from his position as a schoolteacher. I have also helped my own family members through a time of upset over the death of my grandmother, using simple processes. Surprisingly, this brought stability and a sense of calmness, even during this trying time. This is simple technology to use that just makes life easier and much more pleasant for others."

Prior to reading any of Mr. Hubbard's technology, a woman in Hawaii thought the world was full of people who couldn't be trusted. Here is what happened when she learned the true source of the dangers in the environment:

"I realized that I had been looking at everything from someone else's point of view. By changing my point of view, it was a whole different world. It was **not** the world I had previously been taught about at all! This changed so many things for me—I actually started living.

"I was able to observe better, just by looking at what was really there. The environment wasn't so dangerous anymore, not so frightening. I had been taught at a very young age that you must keep your mouth shut and do what you're told and be **very** careful because you can't trust anybody. When I actually **looked,** I found there were a lot of people around me who were good. This opened up my communication because I could say, 'That's not true—look at this, this and that.'

"I used this Scientology data on a radio show. People would call in and ask questions. I got one fellow to realize that he **could** actually make it in life just by observing that others around him were surviving and that he had been fed false information. He is now succeeding in life. His world, like mine, changed from dull gray to a place full of bright colors and enjoyment."

A lady from Germany had the following to say about helping her neighbor:

"Tomorrow was Wednesday, the first Wednesday in the month, when, as always

for the last thirty years, my neighbor comes to my place to discuss all her woes over a cup of coffee. During the years, when our children were still going to school, there used to be concrete problems to discuss and sometimes enjoyable things. Then her husband and children died in a tragic accident. After that, there never was any other subject. But I couldn't just drop her, could I? Come the end of these Wednesday nights, I would be worn out. Another lady had just shown me the way to help someone who is upset. I decided that tomorrow I would take her for walk in the park. And so I did. I broke through her protest about it with cheerful determination. I showed her all my favorite places and discovered quite a few new things myself, and I showed those to her also.

"'Nice out here,' said my neighbor, and I saw her smile for the first time in years."

Sometimes the pressures of the working environment can mount to the point of near overwhelm. A California firm's quality control manager was helped by her boss to regain her composure and return to her job with renewed vigor.

"One day I was totally upset and crying on my job due to who knows what. I couldn't begin to put my finger on what was wrong. All I knew was that I was upset. I couldn't afford to be this way, and neither could others who depended on me. My boss told me to go for a walk and look at things as I walked. I went out and walked for fifteen minutes. I started to feel really good and after a while there actually wasn't any vestige of upset left. When I had started walking, I didn't even know what I was upset about. Yet while I walked, I realized that I had been reluctant to handle one aspect of what I had to do that day. I came up with the solution to the whole problem.

"I turned around, went back and handled the situation totally."

A business consultant of many years' experience has had consistent success in rescuing people from threatening circumstances.

"It's quite common that people who come to me for assistance are living in what they consider to be a dangerous environment. Through letting one little problem or situation after another stack up, unhandled, they soon have a threatening scene indeed. By the time they call me they often have a suffocating mess on their hands, and no apparent way out.

"But there is a way out, of course. Time and again I've had tremendous success using Mr. Hubbard's technique of finding **one** *thing the person can confront and do something about, and getting him or her to really handle* **that.** *The resulting relief, renewed hope and revitalized purpose can be quite something. Getting someone 'back in the game' this way is a rewarding experience."*

An Arizona schoolteacher found a tool far more effective than mere sympathy to help out a co-worker suffering from a lost love.

"One morning one of the other teachers arrived looking unbelievably dismal. It didn't take much questioning to discover

why: His fiancée had left him. It didn't seem possible but by lunchtime his depression had deepened. I shuddered to think what his classes must have been like that morning.

"Some of our friends tried to console him, joke him out of it, and other such well-meaning but ineffective 'solutions' they had probably learned in some psychology class.

*"I pried the fellow away from the others, got him out for a walk around the campus and had him find things in the environment that weren't reminding him of his girlfriend. It wasn't too long before he emerged from his deep gray gloom and started talking about a lecture he had to prepare for, and what he was going to do over the upcoming holiday. A complete change. Saved his day, and saved a lot of students some painful hours listening to someone who wasn't really **there** to teach them."*

About L. Ron Hubbard

No more fitting statement typifies the life of L. Ron Hubbard than his simple declaration: "I like to help others and count it as my greatest pleasure in life to see a person free himself from the shadows which darken his days." Behind these pivotal words stands a lifetime of service to mankind and a legacy of wisdom that enables anyone to attain long-cherished dreams of happiness and spiritual freedom.

Born in Tilden, Nebraska on March 13, 1911, his road of discovery and dedication to his fellows began at an early age. "I wanted other people to be happy, and could not understand why they weren't," he wrote of his youth; and therein lay the sentiments that would long guide his steps. By the age of nineteen, he had traveled more than a quarter of a million miles, examining the cultures of Java, Japan, India and the Philippines.

Returning to the United States in 1929, Ron resumed his formal education and studied mathematics, engineering and the then new field of nuclear physics—all providing vital tools for continued research. To finance that research, Ron embarked upon a literary career in the early 1930s, and soon became one of the most widely read authors of popular fiction. Yet never losing sight of his primary goal, he continued his mainline research through extensive travel and expeditions.

With the advent of World War II, he entered the United States Navy as a lieutenant (junior grade) and served as commander of antisubmarine corvettes. Left partially blind and lame from injuries sustained during combat, he was diagnosed as permanently disabled by 1945. Through application of his theories on the mind, however, he was not only able to help fellow servicemen, but also to regain his own health.

After five more years of intensive research, Ron's discoveries were presented to the world in *Dianetics: The Modern Science of Mental Health*. The first popular handbook on the human mind expressly written for the man in the street, *Dianetics* ushered in a new era of hope for mankind and a new

phase of life for its author. He did, however, not cease his research, and as breakthrough after breakthrough was carefully codified through late 1951, the applied religious philosophy of Scientology was born.

Because Scientology explains the whole of life, there is no aspect of man's existence that L. Ron Hubbard's subsequent work did not address. Residing variously in the United States and England, his continued research brought forth solutions to such social ills as declining educational standards and pandemic drug abuse.

All told, L. Ron Hubbard's works on Scientology and Dianetics total forty million words of recorded lectures, books and writings. Together, these constitute the legacy of a lifetime that ended on January 24, 1986. Yet the passing of L. Ron Hubbard in no way constituted an end; for with a hundred million of his books in circulation and millions of people daily applying his technologies for betterment, it can truly be said the world still has no greater friend.■

Glossary

communication: an interchange of ideas across space between two individuals.

confront: to face without flinching or avoiding. The ability to confront is actually the ability to be there comfortably and perceive.

process: an exact series of directions or sequence of actions taken to accomplish a desired result.

Scientology: an applied religious philosophy developed by L. Ron Hubbard. It is the study and handling of the spirit in relationship to itself, universes and other life. The word *Scientology* comes from the Latin *scio*, which means "know" and the Greek word *logos*, meaning "the word or outward form by which the inward thought is expressed and made known." Thus, Scientology means knowing about knowing.

CHURCHES OF SCIENTOLOGY

Contact Your Nearest Church or Organization
or visit www.volunteerministers.org

UNITED STATES

ALBUQUERQUE
Church of Scientology
8106 Menaul Boulevard NE
Albuquerque, New Mexico 87110

ANN ARBOR
Church of Scientology
66 E. Michigan Avenue
Battle Creek, Michigan 49017

ATLANTA
Church of Scientology
1611 Mt. Vernon Road
Dunwoody, Georgia 30338

AUSTIN
Church of Scientology
2200 Guadalupe
Austin, Texas 78705

BOSTON
Church of Scientology
448 Beacon Street
Boston, Massachusetts 02115

BUFFALO
Church of Scientology
47 West Huron Street
Buffalo, New York 14202

CHICAGO
Church of Scientology
3011 North Lincoln Avenue
Chicago, Illinois 60657-4207

CINCINNATI
Church of Scientology
215 West 4th Street, 5th Floor
Cincinnati, Ohio 45202-2670

CLEARWATER
Church of Scientology
Flag Service Organization
210 South Fort Harrison Avenue
Clearwater, Florida 33756

Foundation Church of
  Scientology
Flag Ship Service Organization
c/o *Freewinds* Relay Office
118 North Fort Harrison Avenue
Clearwater, Florida 33755-4013

COLUMBUS
Church of Scientology
30 North High Street
Columbus, Ohio 43215

DALLAS
Church of Scientology
Celebrity Centre Dallas
1850 North Buckner Boulevard
Dallas, Texas 75228

DENVER
Church of Scientology
3385 South Bannock Street
Englewood, Colorado 80110

DETROIT
Church of Scientology
28000 Middlebelt Road
Farmington Hills, Michigan 48334

HONOLULU
Church of Scientology
1146 Bethel Street
Honolulu, Hawaii 96813

KANSAS CITY
Church of Scientology
3619 Broadway
Kansas City, Missouri 64111

LAS VEGAS
Church of Scientology
846 East Sahara Avenue
Las Vegas, Nevada 89104

Church of Scientology
Celebrity Centre Las Vegas
4850 W. Flamingo Road, Ste. 10
Las Vegas, Nevada 89103

LONG ISLAND
Church of Scientology
99 Railroad Station Plaza
Hicksville, New York 11801-2850

LOS ANGELES AND VICINITY
Church of Scientology
  of Los Angeles
4810 Sunset Boulevard
Los Angeles, California 90027

Church of Scientology
1451 Irvine Boulevard
Tustin, California 92680

Church of Scientology
1277 East Colorado Boulevard
Pasadena, California 91106

Church of Scientology
15643 Sherman Way
Van Nuys, California 91406

Church of Scientology
American Saint Hill
  Organization
1413 L. Ron Hubbard Way
Los Angeles, California 90027

Church of Scientology
American Saint Hill Foundation
1413 L. Ron Hubbard Way
Los Angeles, California 90027

Church of Scientology
Advanced Organization
  of Los Angeles
1306 L. Ron Hubbard Way
Los Angeles, California 90027

Church of Scientology
Celebrity Centre International
5930 Franklin Avenue
Hollywood, California 90028

LOS GATOS
Church of Scientology
2155 South Bascom Avenue,
  Suite 120
Campbell, California 95008

MIAMI
Church of Scientology
120 Giralda Avenue
Coral Gables, Florida 33134

MINNEAPOLIS
Church of Scientology
Twin Cities
1011 Nicollet Mall
Minneapolis, Minnesota 55403

MOUNTAIN VIEW
Church of Scientology
2483 Old Middlefield Way
Mountain View, California 94043

NASHVILLE
Church of Scientology
Celebrity Centre Nashville
1204 16th Avenue South
Nashville, Tennessee 37212

NEW HAVEN
Church of Scientology
909 Whalley Avenue
New Haven, Connecticut
06515-1728

NEW YORK CITY
Church of Scientology
227 West 46th Street
New York, New York 10036-1409

Church of Scientology
Celebrity Centre New York
65 East 82nd Street
New York, New York 10028

ORLANDO
Church of Scientology
1830 East Colonial Drive
Orlando, Florida 32803-4729

PHILADELPHIA
Church of Scientology
1315 Race Street
Philadelphia, Pennsylvania 19107

PHOENIX
Church of Scientology
2111 West University Drive
Mesa, Arizona 85201

PORTLAND
Church of Scientology
2636 NE Sandy Boulevard
Portland, Oregon 97232-2342

Church of Scientology
Celebrity Centre Portland
708 SW Salmon Street
Portland, Oregon 97205

SACRAMENTO
Church of Scientology
825 15th Street
Sacramento, California
95814-2096

SALT LAKE CITY
Church of Scientology
1931 South 1100 East
Salt Lake City, Utah 84106

SAN DIEGO
Church of Scientology
1330 4th Avenue
San Diego, California 92101

SAN FRANCISCO
Church of Scientology
83 McAllister Street
San Francisco, California 94102

SAN JOSE
Church of Scientology
80 East Rosemary Street
San Jose, California 95112

SANTA BARBARA
Church of Scientology
524 State Street
Santa Barbara, California 93101

SEATTLE
Church of Scientology
2226 3rd Avenue
Seattle, Washington 98121

ST. LOUIS
Church of Scientology
6901 Delmar Boulevard
University City, Missouri 63130

TAMPA
Church of Scientology
3617 Henderson Boulevard
Tampa, Florida 33609-4501

WASHINGTON, DC
Founding Church of Scientology
   of Washington, DC
1701 20th Street NW
Washington, DC 20009

PUERTO RICO

HATO REY
Dianetics Center of Puerto Rico
272 JT Piñero Avenue
Hyde Park
San Juan, Puerto Rico 00918

CANADA

EDMONTON
Church of Scientology
10206 106th Street NW
Edmonton, Alberta
Canada T5J 1H7

KITCHENER
Church of Scientology
104 King Street West, 2nd Floor
Kitchener, Ontario
Canada N2G 1A6

MONTREAL
Church of Scientology
4489 Papineau Street
Montreal, Quebec
Canada H2H 1T7

OTTAWA
Church of Scientology
150 Rideau Street, 2nd Floor
Ottawa, Ontario
Canada K1N 5X6

QUEBEC
Church of Scientology
350 Bd Chareste Est
Quebec, Quebec
Canada G1K 3H5

TORONTO
Church of Scientology
696 Yonge Street, 2nd Floor
Toronto, Ontario
Canada M4Y 2A7

VANCOUVER
Church of Scientology
401 West Hastings Street
Vancouver, British Columbia
Canada V6B 1L5

WINNIPEG
Church of Scientology
315 Garry Street, Suite 210
Winnipeg, Manitoba
Canada R3B 2G7

UNITED KINGDOM

BIRMINGHAM
Church of Scientology
8 Ethel Street
Winston Churchill House
Birmingham, England B2 4BG

BRIGHTON
Church of Scientology
Third Floor, 79-83 North Street
Brighton, Sussex
England BN1 1ZA

EAST GRINSTEAD
Church of Scientology
Saint Hill Foundation
Saint Hill Manor
East Grinstead, West Sussex
England RH19 4JY

Advanced Organization
   Saint Hill
Saint Hill Manor
East Grinstead, West Sussex
England RH19 4JY

EDINBURGH
Hubbard Academy of Personal
   Independence
20 Southbridge
Edinburgh, Scotland EH1 1LL

LONDON
Church of Scientology
68 Tottenham Court Road
London, England W1P 0BB

Church of Scientology
Celebrity Centre London
42 Leinster Gardens
London, England W2 3AN

MANCHESTER
Church of Scientology
258 Deansgate
Manchester, England M3 4BG

PLYMOUTH
Church of Scientology
41 Ebrington Street
Plymouth, Devon
England PL4 9AA

SUNDERLAND
Church of Scientology
51 Fawcett Street
Sunderland, Tyne and Wear
England SR1 1RS

AUSTRALIA

ADELAIDE
Church of Scientology
24–28 Waymouth Street
Adelaide, South Australia
Australia 5000

BRISBANE
Church of Scientology
106 Edward Street, 2nd Floor
Brisbane, Queensland
Australia 4000

CANBERRA
Church of Scientology
43–45 East Row
Canberra City, ACT
Australia 2601

MELBOURNE
Church of Scientology
42–44 Russell Street
Melbourne, Victoria
Australia 3000

PERTH
Church of Scientology
108 Murray Street, 1st Floor
Perth, Western Australia
Australia 6000

SYDNEY
Church of Scientology
201 Castlereagh Street
Sydney, New South Wales
Australia 2000

Church of Scientology
Advanced Organization
   Saint Hill Australia,
   New Zealand and Oceania
19–37 Greek Street
Glebe, New South Wales
Australia 2037

NEW ZEALAND

AUCKLAND
Church of Scientology
159 Queen Street, 3rd Floor
Auckland 1, New Zealand

AFRICA

BULAWAYO
Church of Scientology
Southampton House, Suite 202
Main Street and 9th Avenue
Bulawayo, Zimbabwe

CAPE TOWN
Church of Scientology
Ground Floor, Dorlane House
39 Roeland Street
Cape Town 8001, South Africa

DURBAN
Church of Scientology
20 Buckingham Terrace
Westville, Durban 3630
South Africa

HARARE
Church of Scientology
404-409 Pockets Building
50 Jason Moyo Avenue
Harare, Zimbabwe

JOHANNESBURG
Church of Scientology
4th Floor, Budget House
130 Main Street
Johannesburg 2001
South Africa

Church of Scientology
No. 108 1st Floor,
  Bordeaux Centre
Gordon Road, Corner Jan
  Smuts Avenue
Blairgowrie, Randburg 2125
South Africa

PORT ELIZABETH
Church of Scientology
2 St. Christopher's
27 Westbourne Road Central
Port Elizabeth 6001
South Africa

PRETORIA
Church of Scientology
307 Ancore Building
Corner Jeppe and Esselen Streets
Sunnyside, Pretoria 0002
South Africa

SCIENTOLOGY MISSIONS

INTERNATIONAL OFFICE
Scientology Missions
  International
6331 Hollywood Boulevard
  Suite 501
Los Angeles, California
90028-6314

UNITED STATES
Scientology Missions
  International
Western United States Office
1308 L. Ron Hubbard Way
Los Angeles, California 90027

Scientology Missions
  International
Eastern United States Office
349 W. 48th Street
New York, New York 10036

Scientology Missions
  International
Flag Land Base Office
210 South Fort Harrison Avenue
Clearwater, Florida 33756

AFRICA
Scientology Missions
  International
African Office
6th Floor, Budget House
130 Main Street
Johannesburg 2001, South Africa

AUSTRALIA, NEW ZEALAND AND OCEANIA
Scientology Missions
  International
Australian, New Zealand
  and Oceanian Office
201 Castlereagh Street, 3rd Floor
Sydney, New South Wales
Australia 2000

CANADA
Scientology Missions
  International
Canadian Office
696 Yonge Street, 2nd Floor
Toronto, Ontario
Canada M4Y 2A7

UNITED KINGDOM
Scientology Missions
  International
United Kingdom Office
Saint Hill Manor
East Grinstead, West Sussex
England RH19 4JY

TO OBTAIN ANY BOOKS OR CASSETTES BY L. RON HUBBARD WHICH ARE NOT AVAILABLE AT YOUR LOCAL ORGANIZATION, CONTACT ANY OF THE FOLLOWING PUBLICATIONS ORGANIZATIONS WORLDWIDE:

BRIDGE PUBLICATIONS, INC.
4751 Fountain Avenue
Los Angeles, California 90029

www.bridgepub.com

CONTINENTAL PUBLICATIONS LIAISON OFFICE
696 Yonge Street
Toronto, Ontario
Canada M4Y 2A7

NEW ERA PUBLICATIONS INTERNATIONAL ApS
Store Kongensgade 53
1264 Copenhagen K
Denmark

www.newerapublications.com

ERA DINÁMICA EDITORES, S.A. DE C.V.
Pablo Ucello #16
Colonia C.D. de los Deportes
Mexico, D.F.

NEW ERA PUBLICATIONS UK LTD.
Saint Hill Manor
East Grinstead, West Sussex
England RH19 4JY

NEW ERA PUBLICATIONS AUSTRALIA PTY LTD.
Level 1, 61–65 Wentworth
  Avenue
Surry Hills, New South Wales
Australia 2000

CONTINENTAL PUBLICATIONS PTY LTD.
6th Floor, Budget House
130 Main Street
Johannesburg 2001
South Africa

NEW ERA PUBLICATIONS ITALIA S.R.L.
Via Cadorna, 61
20090 Vimodrone (MI), Italy

NEW ERA PUBLICATIONS DEUTSCHLAND GMBH
Hittfelder Kirchweg 5A
21220 Seevetal-Maschen
Germany

NEW ERA PUBLICATIONS FRANCE E.U.R.L.
14, rue des Moulins
75001 Paris, France

NUEVA ERA DINÁMICA, S.A.
C/ Montera 20, 1° dcha.
28013 Madrid, Spain

NEW ERA PUBLICATIONS JAPAN, INC.
Sakai SS bldg 2F, 4-38-15
Higashi-Ikebukuro
Toshima-ku, Tokyo, Japan
170-0013

NEW ERA PUBLICATIONS GROUP
Str. Kasatkina, 16, Building 1
129301 Moscow, Russia

NEW ERA PUBLICATIONS CENTRAL EUROPEAN OFFICE
1438 Budapest
Pf. 351
Hungary

BUILD A BETTER WORLD
BECOME A VOLUNTEER MINISTER

Help bring happiness, purpose and truth to your fellow man. Become a Volunteer Minister.

Thousands of Volunteer Ministers bring relief and sanity to others all over the world using techniques like the ones found in this booklet. But more help is needed. Your help.

As a Volunteer Minister you can today handle things which seemed impossible yesterday. And you can vastly improve this world's tomorrow.

Become a Volunteer Minister and brighten the world to a better place for you to live. It's easy to do. For help and information about becoming a Volunteer Minister, visit our website today. www.volunteerministers.org

You can also call or write your nearest Volunteer Ministers International organization.

VOLUNTEER MINISTERS INTERNATIONAL
A DEPARTMENT OF THE INTERNATIONAL HUBBARD ECCLESIASTICAL LEAGUE OF PASTORS

INTERNATIONAL OFFICE
6331 Hollywood Boulevard, Suite 708
Los Angeles, California 90028
Tel: (323) 960-3560 (800) 435-7498

WESTERN US
1308 L. Ron Hubbard Way
Los Angeles, California 90027
Tel: (323) 953-3357
1-888-443-5760
ihelpwestus@earthlink.net

EASTERN US
349 W. 48th Street
New York, New York 10036
Tel: (212) 757-9610
1-888-443-5788

CANADA
696 Yonge Street
Toronto, Ontario
Canada M4Y 2A7
Tel: (416) 968-0070

LATIN AMERICA
Federación Mexicana de
Dianética, A.C.
Puebla #31
Colonia Roma, CP 06700
Mexico, D.F.
Tel: 525-511-4452

EUROPE
Store Kongensgade 55
1264 Copenhagen K
Denmark
Tel: 45-33-737-322

ITALY
Via Cadorna, 61
20090 Vimodrone (MI)
Italy
Tel: 39-0227-409-246

AUSTRALIA
201 Castlereagh Street
3rd Floor
Sydney, New South Wales
Australia 2000
Tel: 612-9267-6422

AFRICA
6th Floor, Budget House
130 Main Street
Johannesburg 2001
South Africa
Tel: 083-331-7170

UNITED KINGDOM
Saint Hill Manor
East Grinstead, West Sussex
England RH19 4JY
Tel: 44-1342-301-895

HUNGARY
1438 Budapest
PO Box 351, Hungary
Tel: 361-321-5298

COMMONWEALTH OF INDEPENDENT STATES
c/o Hubbard Humanitarian
Center
Ul. Borisa Galushkina 19A
129301 Moscow, Russia
Tel: 7-095-961-3414

TAIWAN
2F, 65, Sec. 4
Ming-Sheng East Road
Taipei, Taiwan ROC
Tel: 88-628-770-5074

www.volunteerministers.org

Bridge Publications, Inc.
4751 Fountain Avenue, Los Angeles, CA 90029
ISBN 0-88404-919-1

©1994, 2001 L. Ron Hubbard Library. All Rights Reserved. Any unauthorized copying, translation, duplication, importation or distribution, in whole or in part, by any means, including electronic copying, storage or transmission, is a violation of applicable laws.

Scientology, Dianetics, Celebrity Centre, L. Ron Hubbard, Flag, Freewinds, the L. Ron Hubbard Signature, the Scientology Cross (rounded) and the Scientology Cross (pointed) are trademarks and service marks owned by Religious Technology Center and are used with its permission. *Scientologist* is a collective membership mark designating members of the affiliated churches and missions of Scientology.

NEW ERA is a trademark and service mark.

Bridge Publications, Inc. is a registered trademark and service mark in California and it is owned by Bridge Publications, Inc.

Printed in the United States of America

An L. RON HUBBARD Publication